A CENTURY *of*
BIRMINGHAM

The Bull Ring, *c.* 1950. (*Birmingham Central Library, Warwickshire Photographic Survey*)

A CENTURY *of* BIRMINGHAM

PATRICK BAIRD

SUTTON PUBLISHING

First published in the United Kingdom in 2000 by Sutton Publishing Limited

This new paperback edition first published in 2007 by
Sutton Publishing, an imprint of NPI Media Group
Cirencester Road · Chalford · Stroud · Gloucestershire · GL6 8PE

British Library Cataloguing in Publication Data
A catalogue record for this book is available from the British Library.

ISBN 978-0-7509-4945-3

Front endpaper: New Street Station, 1900. *(John Whybrow Collection)*
Back endpaper: New Summer Street, 1934. *(Birmingham Central Library, Warwickshire Photographic Survey)*
Half title page: Street theatre near Colmore Row. *(Birmingham Central Library, Warwickshire Photographic Survey)*
Title page: Bull Ring and the Rotunda, 1964. *(Birmingham Central Library, Warwickshire Photographic Survey)*

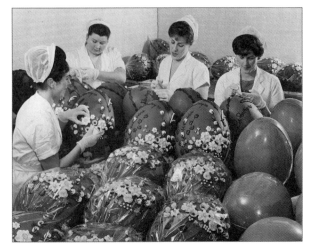

Typeset in Photina.
Typesetting and origination by
Sutton Publishing.
Printed and bound in England.

Decorating Easter eggs at Cadbury's, Bournville, 1960s. *(Birmingham Central Library, Warwickshire Photographic Survey)*

Contents

The Woodman, Easy Row, 1964. (*Birmingham Central Library, Warwickshire Photographic Survey*)

Foreword

I am delighted that you are producing a book celebrating the events and people of Birmingham.

Birmingham has had a fascinating history, and much of it packed into the last century, when photography became an important and valuable tool for documenting  fleeting times. This book helps us remember the colourful characters this unique city has produced over the years. Birmingham is home to one million people and they are from many diverse cultures and backgrounds. This is the strength of the city, a mixture that produces a multitude of skills and talents. The drive for innovation, the constant search for 'the new', has kept Birmingham young and vibrant, with eyes fixed on the horizon and the next opportunity.

Photography in the last century has moved from its infancy into a golden age, and on into the new high tech world of digital computer-driven images. This could be taken as a metaphor for Birmingham itself as it strives to re-invent itself yet again, expanding from its historical manufacturing base and establishing itself as an important player in other, developing worlds such as commerce and tourism.

Councillor Theresa Stewart
Lord Mayor of Birmingham

A trip to the Museum of Science and Industry, Newhall Street, 1973. (*Birmingham Central Library, Warwickshire Photographic Survey*)

Britain: A Century
of Change

Two women encumbered with gas masks go about their daily tasks during the early days of the war. (*Hulton Getty Picture Collection*)

The sixty years ending in 1900 were a period of huge transformation for Britain. Railway stations, post-and-telegraph offices, police and fire stations, gasworks and gasometers, new livestock markets and covered markets, schools, churches, football grounds, hospitals and asylums, water pumping stations and sewerage plants totally altered the urban scene, and the country's population tripled with more than seven out of ten people being born in or moving to the towns. The century that followed, leading up to the Millennium's end in 2000, was to be a period of even greater change.

When Queen Victoria died in 1901, she was measured for her coffin by her grandson Kaiser Wilhelm, the London prostitutes put on black mourning and the blinds came down in the villas and terraces spreading out from the old town centres. These centres were reachable by train and tram, by the new bicycles and still newer motor cars, were connected by the new telephone, and lit by gas or even electricity. The shops may have been full of British-made cotton and woollen clothing but the grocers and butchers were selling cheap Danish bacon, Argentinian beef, Australasian mutton and tinned or dried fish and fruit from Canada, California and South Africa. Most of these goods were carried in British-built-and-crewed ships burning Welsh steam coal.

As the first decade moved on, the Open Spaces Act meant more parks, bowling greens and cricket pitches. The First World War transformed the place of women, as they took over many men's jobs. Its other legacies were the war memorials which joined the statues of Victorian worthies in main squares round the land. After 1918 death duties and higher taxation bit hard, and a quarter of England changed hands in the space of only a few years.

The multiple shop – the chain store – appeared in the high street: Sainsburys, Maypole, Lipton's, Home & Colonial, the Fifty Shilling Tailor, Burton, Boots, W.H. Smith. The shopper was spoilt for choice, attracted by the brash fascias and advertising hoardings for national brands like Bovril, Pears Soap, and Ovaltine. Many new buildings began to be seen, such as garages, motor showrooms, picture palaces (cinemas), 'palais de dance', and ribbons of 'semis' stretched along the roads and new bypasses and onto the new estates nudging the green belts.

During the 1920s cars became more reliable and sophisticated as well as commonplace, with developments like the electric self-starter making them easier for women to drive. Who wanted to turn a crank handle in the new short skirt? This was, indeed, the electric age as much as the motor era. Trolley buses, electric trams and trains extended mass transport and electric light replaced gas in the street and the home, which itself was groomed by the vacuum cleaner.

A major jolt to the march onward and upward was administered by the Great Depression of the early 1930s. The older British industries

– textiles, shipbuilding, iron, steel, coal – were already under pressure from foreign competition when this worldwide slump arrived. Luckily there were new diversions to alleviate the misery. The 'talkies' arrived in the cinemas; more and more radios and gramophones were to be found in people's homes; there were new women's magazines, with fashion, cookery tips and problem pages; football pools; the flying feats of women pilots like Amy Johnson; the Loch Ness Monster; cheap chocolate and the drama of Edward VIII's abdication.

Things were looking up again by 1936 and new light industry was booming in the Home Counties as factories struggled to keep up with the demand for radios, radiograms, cars and electronic goods, including the first television sets. The threat from Hitler's Germany meant rearmament, particularly of the airforce, which stimulated aircraft and aero engine firms. If you were lucky and lived in the south, there was good money to be earned. A semi-detached house cost £450, a Morris Cowley £150. People may have smoked like chimneys but life expectancy, since 1918, was up by 15 years while the birth rate had almost halved.

A W.H.Smith shop front in Beaconsfield, 1922.

In some ways it is the little memories that seem to linger longest from the Second World War: the kerbs painted white to show up in the blackout, the rattle of ack-ack shrapnel on roof tiles, sparrows killed by bomb blast. The biggest damage, apart from London, was in the south-west (Plymouth, Bristol) and the Midlands (Coventry, Birmingham). Postwar reconstruction was rooted in the Beveridge Report which set out the expectations for the Welfare State. This, together with the nationalisation of the Bank of England, coal, gas, electricity and the railways, formed the programme of the Labour government in 1945.

Children collecting aluminium to help the war effort, London, 1940s. (*IWM*)

Times were hard in the late 1940s, with rationing even more stringent than during the war. Yet this was, as has been said, 'an innocent and well-behaved era'. The first let-up came in 1951 with the Festival of Britain and there was another fillip in 1953 from the Coronation, which incidentally gave a huge boost to the spread of TV. By 1954 leisure motoring had been resumed but the Comet – Britain's best hope for taking on the American aviation industry – suffered a series of mysterious crashes. The Suez debacle of 1956 was followed by an acceleration in the withdrawal from Empire, which had begun in 1947 with the Independence of India. Consumerism was truly born with the advent of commercial TV and most homes soon boasted washing machines, fridges, electric irons and fires.

A street party to celebrate the Queen's Coronation, June 1953. (*Hulton Getty Picture Collection*)

The *Lady Chatterley* obscenity trial in 1960 was something of a straw in the wind for what was to follow in that decade. A collective loss of inhibition seemed to sweep the land, as the Beatles and the Rolling Stones transformed popular music, and retailing, cinema and the theatre were revolutionised. Designers, hairdressers, photographers and models moved into places vacated by an Establishment put to flight by the new breed of satirists spawned by *Beyond the Fringe* and *Private Eye*.

In the 1970s Britain seems to have suffered a prolonged hangover after the excesses of the previous decade. Ulster, inflation and union troubles were not made up for by entry into the EEC, North Sea Oil, Women's Lib or, indeed, Punk Rock. Mrs Thatcher applied the corrective in the 1980s, as the country moved more and more from its old manufacturing base over to providing services, consulting, advertising, and expertise in the 'invisible' market of high finance or in IT.

The post-1945 townscape has seen changes to match those in the worlds of work, entertainment and politics. In 1952 the Clean Air Act served notice on smogs and pea-souper fogs, smuts and blackened buildings, forcing people to stop burning coal and go over to smokeless sources of heat and energy. In the same decade some of the best urban building took place in the 'new towns' like Basildon, Crawley, Stevenage and Harlow. Elsewhere open warfare was declared on slums and what was labelled inadequate, cramped, back-to-back, two-up, two-down, housing. The new 'machine for living in' was a flat in a high-rise block. The architects and planners who promoted these were in league with the traffic engineers, determined to keep the motor car moving whatever the price in multi-storey car parks, meters, traffic wardens and ring roads. The old pollutant, coal smoke, was replaced by petrol and diesel exhaust, and traffic noise.

Punk rockers demonstrate their anarchic style during the 1970s. (*Barnaby's Picture Library*)

Fast food was no longer only a pork pie in a pub or fish-and-chips. There were Indian curry houses, Chinese take-aways and American-style hamburgers, while the drinker could get away from beer in a wine bar. Under the impact of television the big Gaumonts and Odeons closed or were rebuilt as multi-screen cinemas, while the palais de dance gave way to discos and clubs.

From the late 1960s the introduction of listed buildings and conservation areas, together with the growth of preservation societies, put a brake on 'comprehensive redevelopment'. The end of the century and the start of the Third Millennium see new challenges to the health of towns and the wellbeing of the nine out of ten people who now live urban lives. The fight is on to prevent town centres from dying, as patterns of housing and shopping change, and edge-of-town supermarkets exercise the attractions of one-stop shopping. But as banks and department stores close, following the haberdashers, greengrocers, butchers and ironmongers, there are signs of new growth such as farmers' markets, and corner stores acting as pick-up points where customers collect shopping ordered on-line from web sites.

Millennium celebrations over the Thames
at Westminster, New Year's Eve, 1999.
(*Barnaby's Picture Library*)

Futurologists tell us that we are in stage two of the consumer revolution: a shift from mass consumption to mass customisation driven by
a desire to have things that fit us and our particular lifestyle exactly,
and for better service. This must offer hope for small city-centre shop
premises, as must the continued attraction of physical shopping,
browsing and being part of a crowd: in a word, 'shoppertainment'.
Another hopeful trend for towns is the growth in the number of young
people postponing marriage and looking to live independently, alone,
where there is a buzz, in 'swinging single cities'. Theirs is a 'flats-and-
cafés' lifestyle, in contrast to the 'family suburbs', and certainly fits in
with government's aim of building 60 per cent of the huge amount of
new housing needed on 'brown' sites, recycled urban land. There looks
to be plenty of life in the British town yet.

Birmingham: An Introduction

Since the Middle Ages Birmingham has played a significant part in the history of the industrialisation of England. Indeed in 1693 Alexander Missen in his *Travels* concluded that he saw in Milan 'fine works of rock crystal, swords, heads of canes, snuff boxes and other fine works of steel – but they could be had better and cheaper in Birmingham.'

By the arrival of the eighteenth century the rapidly expanding town was leading the development of the Industrial Revolution in this country. Making their bases here were the now famous leading industrial characters, Matthew Boulton, James Watt and William Murdoch. From this early expansion the industries continued to grow until, in the nineteenth century, the town became known as 'the city of a thousand trades.' Evidence of the vast amount of items manufactured in the town can be found in a calculation taken at the very end of the century giving the result of a single week's production:

> 14,000,000 steel pens, 6,000 bedsteads, 7,000 guns, 300,000 cut nails, 100,000,000 buttons, 5,000,000 copper or bronze coins, 20,000 pairs of spectacles, 6 tons of papier maché ware, £30,000 worth of jewellery, 4,000 miles of iron and steel wire, 16 tons of pins, 5 tons of hair pins, hooks and eyes, 130,000 gross wood screws, and 500 tons of nuts and bolts.

Two of the major industries within this list which have been major assets to Birmingham are the jewellery and gun manufacturing trades. There is no date upon which to base the beginning of jewellery making in the town but at the start of the nineteenth century it is probable that some 400 artisans were employed in ten or twelve manufactories: those working in gold made seals, keys and watch chains, whilst the silver workers produced shoe, knee and other buckles as well as considerable numbers of comb ornaments. The discovery of gold in Australia and California, the increased wealth of England and her colonies, together with the desire for personal adornment, later united to give an unparalleled prosperity to the industry, which by the middle of the nineteenth century, directly and indirectly gave employment to a larger number of people than any other trade in Birmingham. Even today the 'jewellery quarter' in Hockley, with its vast number of small workshops and retail outlets is an important tourist attraction and includes the Museum of the Jewellery Quarter – the former jewellery factory of Smith and Pepper – in its original state.

Guns were produced in considerable quantities in Birmingham by the middle of the seventeenth century but is difficult to trace when they were first made. There is some reason to believe that someone called Hadley produced the first gun but local tradition has long preserved a version that King William III was regretting the fact that no guns were made in England and received a reply from Sir Richard Newdigate, MP for Warwickshire, that 'The men of Birmingham can do whatever skill and metal can do'. This consequently led to a number of Birmingham workers producing guns for the King – guns that he was well satisfied with – and the beginnings of the Birmingham gun trade. Its greatest peak of success was attained during the Crimean War (when the Birmingham Small Arms Company (BSA) was formed) and the American Civil War, when production of firearms was enormous, with the consequence that fortunes were amassed by manufacturers.

Today those who do not know the city regard it as 'a big, brash, dirty industrial city whose people are rough and talk with an unbearable nasal accent' – an impression which is not justified. As well as the fame achieved for its industrial acumen, Birmingham also has a fine reputation for music and the arts. For nearly 150 years a music festival, held once every three years, attracted the most famous composers and musicians of the day, including Mendelssohn, who wrote the oratorio *Elijah* for the 1846 festival, and Birmingham's own adopted Edward Elgar who, for the 1900 festival, wrote the music for *Dream of Gerontius*. Today it is home to the world-renowned City of Birmingham Symphony Orchestra.

The first reference to Birmingham can be found in the Domesday survey of 1086 where an estimate of what the whole area could be worth was 20 shillings (£1). For centuries the town was little more than the present town centre. Expansion came with the addition of Balsall Heath in 1866, followed by Harborne in 1891. It was not until 1911, following advice from the Boundaries

Lily Place, Gem Street, 1930. One of the many courts/back-to-back housing which were so prevalent in Birmingham during the nineteenth century. Gem Street was situated in the area now occupied by part of the University of Aston. (*Birmingham Central Library, Warwickshire Photographic Survey*)

Commission, that the Greater Birmingham Extension Act added to the town the manors of Aston, Handsworth, Erdington, Kings Norton and Yardley. This trebled the size of the city at one great swoop. Birmingham was granted a city charter in 1889.

Following the First World War, the need for adequate housing remained a great challenge and a number of major municipal housing estates were developed in the areas annexed to the city in 1911, turning rural scenes into sprawling suburbia. The clearance of the city centre slums was finally achieved after the Second World War.

The Second World War itself brought over eighty major air raids on the city, killing 2,000 and injuring 3,000 people. Much of the city centre was destroyed and much damage done to essential industries, but the spirit of the people of Birmingham was unbeaten.

By the beginning of the 1970s, manufacturing industries were still holding their own but in 1973 one of the major ones, the Birmingham Small Arms Company (BSA) went into liquidation and more recently the biggest manufacturing plant in Birmingham, BMW/Rover (originally Austin Motor Company and later British Leyland), was put up for sale and there was danger of closure with the possible disappearance of up to 50,000 jobs in the region. With the emergence of the Phoenix group it is hoped the plant will go forward into a period of stability and advance.

The move now is away from manufacturing towards service-based industries, particularly in bars, hotels and restaurants, which are thriving following the coming of the International Convention Centre, Symphony Hall, Brindley Place, the National Indoor Arena, the National Exhibition Centre and the forthcoming 'Mailbox' project. The National Exhibition Centre attracts many major exhibitions and has extended considerably since its opening. It is on an ideal site at the crossroads of the motorways, with the airport and railway station adjacent to it. Employing many people, it now ranks as one of the major exhibition centres in Europe.

Central Library and Midland Institute, 1962. The original library in Ratcliff Place was designed by William Martin (with elevation by E.M. Barry) and opened in 1866. However, on 11 January 1879, a fire broke out and the library was reduced to a black and smouldering heap; only 100 of its stock of 50,000 volumes were saved. A new building was designed almost immediately afterwards and opened on 1 June 1882, remaining until the early 1970s when the current building was completed.

The Birmingham and Midland Institute, an Italianate design by E.M. Barry, was constructed in the 1850s but demolished in the 1960s. The Institute, however, still flourishes and has its offices in Margaret Street. Since its inception it has had many famous personalities as its Presidents, including Charles Dickens, André Maurois and, more recently, Fay Weldon. (*Birmingham Central Library, Warwickshire Photographic Survey*)

Redevelopment of the city centre after the Second World War saw the construction of the Bull Ring Centre and the Inner Ring Road. Houses gave way to high rise flats, including two 32-storey blocks at Lea Hall. This idea was later much regretted by public and planners alike.

The next stage forward over the coming few years will see the demolition and redevelopment of the Bull Ring and the development of the Eastside projects to complete a fine city design that began so well with the Broad Street developments in the early 1990s.

Birmingham is a diverse cultural community enriched by peoples from all over the world making it their home. The Irish have certainly been here since the coming of the railways in the 1840s, and were possibly here a century earlier when the canals were constructed. Italians from the southern region of Lazio have also been in the city since the mid-nineteenth century – making their 'little Italy' home in the area around Jennens Row, Fazeley Street and New Canal Street. Another substantial group are the Chinese, some of whom arrived during the First World War to work in factories and remained to build up a substantial business in restaurants and supermarkets, thus creating 'Chinatown' near to the Arcadian centre and the Hippodrome theatre. A more recent influx of colonial immigrants, including peoples from the Indian sub-continent and Afro-Caribbean countries, means that Birmingham now has the largest ethnic percentage of population in the UK – almost 25 per cent.

Birmingham people have always taken the time to enjoy themselves. Not all could afford to go on holiday, but a coach or 'charabanc' trip to Weston-Super-Mare, Rhyl or Weymouth was very popular. Those who could not afford the expense could take a tram along the beautiful tree-lined Bristol Road to the Lickey Hills – a beauty spot on the south side of the city given freely by the Cadbury family, or travel to Sutton Park just over the city boundary. They may even have gone further, taking a bus or train from the Bull Ring to Stratford-upon-Avon to spend a happy day picnicking beside the River Avon, admiring the riverside gardens, taking a motor boat trip, or just wandering through the streets of the town. Today far-flung places are the more likely holiday destinations.

So from those early days the city has grown, become known worldwide and today goes, as its coat of arms says, 'Forward' with confidence into the future.

Floods at Digbeth, 1982. Until the nineteenth century, flooding was prevalent in the Digbeth area because of its low-lying situation and its closeness to the River Rea. Following the culverting of the river flooding virtually came to a stop although occasional occurrences did happen. However, this one may have been the result of a burst water main. (*Birmingham Central Library, Warwickshire Photographic Survey*)

At the Dawn of the Twentieth Century

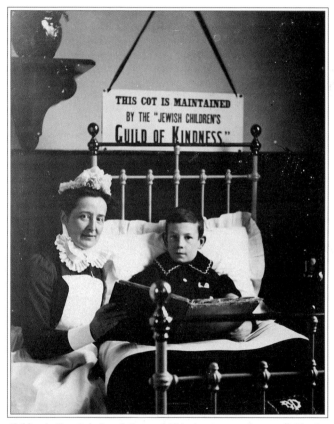

Children's Hospital, Broad Street, 1904. A nurse reads to a child who lies in a cot maintained by the 'Jewish Children's Guild of Kindness'. The hospital later moved to a new building in Ladywood, named in memory of the late King Edward VII, which opened in December 1917. *(Birmingham Central Library, Warwickshire Photographic Survey)*

Celebrations outside the City Museum and Art Gallery, Chamberlain Square, marking the end of the Boer War in 1902. Over 270 Birmingham men died in the war, mainly from diseases such as dysentery and enteric fever. This photograph was taken by a well-known woman photographer in the area – Mary W. Neale. (*Birmingham Central Library, Warwickshire Photographic Survey*)

Gypsy encampment at the Black Patch near Hockley Brook, between Hockley and Handsworth, at the turn of the nineteenth century. The camp existed for many years. However, all but the very oldest gypsies were turned off in 1905. (*Birmingham Central Library, Warwickshire Photographic Survey*)

Henty, Queen of the Gypsies, at the Black Patch, 1900. Henty and a few others, who had lived there for twenty or twenty-five years or more, were allowed to remain until after the Queen's death which occurred in 1907. (*Birmingham Central Library, Warwickshire Photographic Survey*)

Group of political workers at The Grange, the home of John Benjamin Stone, MP for East Birmingham, 1901. Stone's hobby was to tour the world taking photographs and more than 22,000 of these are housed at Birmingham Central Library. He died in July 1906, followed by his wife (who was seriously ill and unaware of his death) four days later. They were buried together at Sutton Coldfield. *(Birmingham Central Library, Benjamin Stone Collection)*

Mr F.H. Pepper and his children making a morning call at the Grange, 1903. Note the early motor. Mr Pepper was a pioneer in the early days of the motor car and became a director of the Austin Motor Car Company. *(Birmingham Central Library, Benjamin Stone Collection)*

Before the beginning of the century, Birmingham had become known as 'The City of 1,000 Trades', since virtually anything man-made was manufactured here. This photograph shows the forging of bedsteads in 1902 at a successful bed manufacturers – Fisher, Brown and Bayley Ltd, of Lionel Street. *(Birmingham Central Library, Warwickshire Photographic Survey)*

Market Hall, Bull Ring, between Philip Street and Bell Street. The market hall opened in 1835 and this shows the fish and game stalls on the left and dining stalls on the right in 1901. The interior was completely burned out by enemy action on the night of 25/26 August 1940. Its exterior walls were later demolished to make way for the Bull Ring Shopping Centre. *(Birmingham Central Library, Warwickshire Photographic Survey)*

23

Birmingham society wedding of Edwin Elliott and Amy Winifred Turner, 25 July 1908. The photograph was taken in the garden of Rotton Park Lodge, Edgbaston, after a service at Francis Road Congregational Church, Edgbaston. Edwin Elliott founded E. Elliott, plastic moulders, in 1935 and later acquired control of the British Optical Lens Company which he expanded. He did not retire until the age of eighty-eight in 1966. *(Miss Margery Elliott)*

Children at the site of the new Blue Coat School, Harborne, 19 August 1913. The Blue Coat School had been founded in 1722 to give orphans, and the children of the poor, clothing maintenance, a good elementary education and religious instruction according to the principles of the Church of England. The original buildings stood close to Colmore Row near St Philip's Church (now the Cathedral) and were opened in 1724. In 1913 land was purchased at a site at the junction of Harborne Hill and Metchley Lane, extending along Somerset Road at Harborne but, because of difficulties selling the site together with the intervention of the First World War, the building was not completed until 1930. (*Birmingham Central Library, Benjamin Stone Collection*)

Girls in a classroom at Mason's Orphanage, Erdington, 1908. The orphanage was founded by Kidderminster-born Josiah Mason (1795–1881) who moved to Birmingham and made his fortune in pen manufacture. He founded an orphanage in Erdington in the 1860s and the Scientific College at Birmingham (Edmund Street) in 1880. This was later upgraded to university status in 1900. The orphanage was demolished in 1964. (*Birmingham Central Library, Benjamin Stone Collection*)

Birmingham University (The Great Hall) under construction, 1908. In 1901 Joseph Chamberlain instructed architects Aston Webb and Ingress Bell to design buildings for a new site acquired at Edgbaston Park Road. A full programme of building was set in motion in 1904. (*Birmingham Central Library, Benjamin Stone Collection*)

Interior of the power station at Birmingham University, 1908. This was the first university building ready for use and its first engine required to give heat and light was set in motion in 1904. (*Birmingham Central Library, Benjamin Stone Collection*)

Temple Row looking towards Colmore Row decorated for the visit of King Edward VII when he visited Birmingham to open the university buildings on 7 July 1909. *(Birmingham Central Library, Warwickshire Photographic Survey)*

Celebrations for the 70th birthday of Joseph Chamberlain at Ward End Park on 7 July 1906. Chamberlain (1836–1914) was probably Birmingham's favourite politician. Having given the city domestic gas and electricity, he celebrated with the people by taking part in a motorcade and stroll through at least two of Birmingham's parks. He is seen here in top hat with his third wife, American heiress Mary Endicott, on his right. *(Birmingham Central Library, Benjamin Stone Collection)*

As late as 1915, a good deal of the Birmingham area was agricultural rather than urban. This photograph is of Thomas Reeves, resting from his work as a farmer at Tritterford Farm, Yardley Wood. *(Birmingham Central Library, Warwickshire Photographic Survey)*

A group of farmers/workers standing on the site of Yardley Wood School, *c.* 1905. Left to right: Frank Holt, Thomas Reeves, Ted Reeves and Tom Taylor from Warstock Farm. *(Birmingham Central Library, Warwickshire Photographic Survey)*

House back of 2 Berkley Street (near Gas Street, Suffolk Street), *c.* 1905. Not everyone living in the city had a reasonable lifestyle as this shows. The area from the centre towards Ladywood was overladen with back-to-backs and slums similar to these. Luckily many were improved or demolished shortly after this photograph was taken. *(Birmingham Central Library, Slum Collection)*

Buffalo Bill's visit to Birmingham, in 1903. Buffalo Bill (William F. Cody) and his circus visited Birmingham in 1887, 1891, 1903 and 1917. Here, in 1903, an American Indian Chief and braves parade down New Street towards Corporation Street. *(Birmingham Central Library, Buffalo Bill Collection)*

News vendor noting the 'Lloyd George Riots', 1901. On 18 December a pro-Boer meeting was held at the Town Hall. Lloyd George was present to protest against the war. Passions ran high and, according to one witness, 'a howling mob of well-nigh a 100,000 outraged patriots stormed the Town Hall'. One man was killed and Lloyd George was forced to leave the building but the only way he could do so without forfeiting his life was in the disguise of a policeman. *(Birmingham Central Library, Warwickshire Photographic Survey)*

A street scavenger in Paradise Street cleaning up horse droppings, 1903. In the background what eventually became known as 'Galloways Corner' is being constructed. *(Birmingham Central Library, Warwickshire Photographic Survey)*

The last horse sale in the Horse Fair, Bristol Street, 1911. A regular horse sale had begun in Ann Street (now Colmore Row) and moved to the area of Bristol Street known as the Horse Fair in the eighteenth century. *(Birmingham Central Library, Warwickshire Photographic Survey)*

Charles Gore (1853–1932). First Anglican Bishop of Birmingham (1905–11). A forceful character, he established excellent relations with the civic authorities, with free churchmen and with evangelicals. His eloquence on care for the true progress of a great city won him a remarkable position in its public life. He left Birmingham in 1911 to become Bishop of Oxford. (*Birmingham Central Library, Portraits Collection*)

The First World War

William Henry Bowater was elected Lord Mayor in 1914 following the
resignation of Ernest Martineau who had volunteered for active service
abroad. Bowater had previously been Lord Mayor between 1909 and 1912,
during and after the extension of the city and he led Birmingham into
wartime activity. He set up the Citizens' Committee, collected large sums
of money for war purposes and accompanied King George V on his visit
to local munitions factories in July 1915. For these deeds he received the
thanks of the Army Council and was made an Honorary Colonel, created a
Knight and received the Freedom of the City. (*Birmingham Central Library,
Portraits Collection*)

2nd City Battalion (Birmingham) Royal Warwickshire Regiment leaving Sutton Coldfield for training in Yorkshire, July 1915. *(Birmingham Central Library, Warwickshire Photographic Survey)*

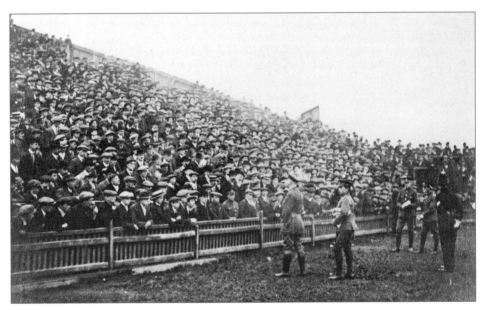

Recruiting meeting held at St Andrew's Football Ground (home of Birmingham City Football Club), 1914. Major John Hall-Edwards (pioneer of X-rays in the United Kingdom) is addressing the crowd. *(Birmingham Central Library, Warwickshire Photographic Survey)*

Mills Munitions Company, Bridge Street West, *c.* 1916. The famous Mills hand grenade was invented here and produced in hundreds of thousands, mainly by women workers. (*Birmingham Central Library, World War One Collection*)

Mills Munitions Company, *c.* 1916. Assessing hand grenades and demonstrating air test for tightness of powder. *(Birmingham Central Library, World War One Collection)*

Happy smiling women workers at one of the many factories producing munitions in the First World War, *c.* 1915. One startling statistic shows that, from May 1915 to the end of the war, a total of 15,000,000 munitions were manufactured – enough to fill a train stretching from Birmingham to Bournemouth. *(University of Birmingham, Chinn Collection)*

Highbury, Moseley – the former home of Joseph Chamberlain – which, after his death in July 1914, was no longer used as a family home. During the First World War it was taken over and used as an annexe to the First Southern General Hospital (based at Birmingham University) and later a home for disabled ex-servicemen. *(Birmingham Central Library, Highbury Collection)*

Servicemen recuperating at Highbury, *c.* 1917. *(Birmingham Central Library, Highbury Collection)*

Sergeant E.M. Tissies of the 15th Canadians and Sergeant G. West, both of whom were evidently patients at Highbury in 1917. How interesting it would be if anyone recognises them and could throw some light on their later lives. *(Birmingham Central Library, Highbury Collection)*

Dorothy Fuller, originally from Devon, who came to Birmingham to work as a tram conductress during the First World War. She was based at the Coventry Road Depot where she met her husband to be – a tram driver. *(University of Birmingham, Chinn Collection)*

The Great Hall at Birmingham University, *c.* 1914. The Hall was used as the principal ward of the First Southern General Hospital. By the end of the war over 67,000 patients had been treated. *(Birmingham Central Library, Warwickshire Photographic Survey)*

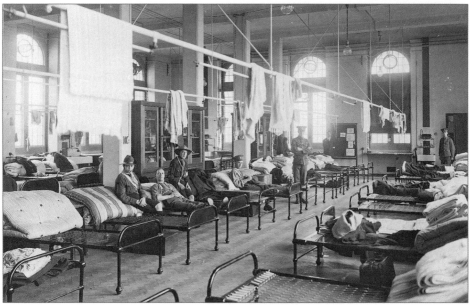

First Southern General Hospital, University of Birmingham, 1914. Physics Block turned into barracks. *(Birmingham Central Library, Warwickshire Photographic Survey)*

Birmingham Tank Week, 31 December
1917–5 January 1918. This was part of a
national campaign conducted by local war savings
committees to get people to put their money into
wartime accounts. Several tanks visited towns and
cities throughout the UK and often caused great
excitement as very few people had seen a tank close
up, never mind inside. *(Birmingham Central Library,
Warwickshire Photographic Survey)*

Thorp Street Barracks, Birmingham. Welcome of the 1/6 Royal Warwickshire Regiment on its return from Italy by A.D. Brooks, Lord Mayor 1918. *(Birmingham Central Library, World War One Collection)*

Street party in Birchwood Road, Sparkbrook, celebrating the end of the First World War, 1919. *(University of Birmingham, Chinn Collection)*

First sale of whisky after the war. Queues build up outside the premises of E.H. James, wine merchants, at Dale End, 1918. *(Birmingham Central Library, World War One Collection)*

Wartime symphony concert held at the Town Hall, 10 October 1917. In the centre of the rostrum is Sir Thomas Beecham, to the left is A.D. Brooks, Lord Mayor of Birmingham, and on the right is Neville Chamberlain, former Lord Mayor and later Prime Minister. *(Birmingham Central Library, World War One Collection)*

Balmy Days and Stormy Nights

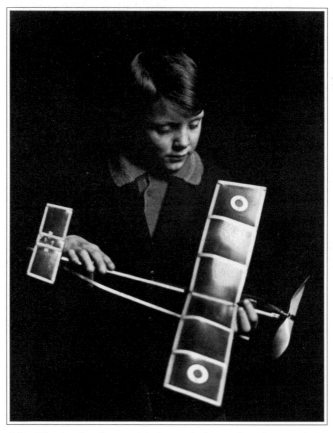

Colin Whitehead with a model plane, which may have been made by himself. The photograph was taken by his father, L.D. Whitehead, in 1928. *(Mrs Jean Smith)*

Smiling crowds enjoy a goodwill visit by King George V and Queen Mary as they drive through Selly Oak on a day which included a visit to Cadbury Bros at Bournville, 1919. The King can be seen in his military uniform. *(Birmingham Central Library, Miscellaneous Collection)*

One of the many popular charabanc tours organised by offices, factories and groups. This one was organised by the Birmingham Co-op and shows many associated members of the AEW union setting out from Birmingham to Evesham. *c.* 1925. *(Birmingham Central Library, Miscellaneous Collection)*

The Hall of Memory, Broad Street, *c.* 1926. Designed by S.N. Cooke and W.N. Twist and built of Portland stone, this building originally commemorated those Birmingham people who were killed serving in the First World War. A remembrance book inside lists names and now includes those 'Brummies' killed in all wars since. (*Birmingham Central Library, Warwickshire Photographic Survey*)

The opening of the Hall of Memory by HRH Prince Arthur of Connaught, 4 July 1925. Seen in the mayoral robes is Alderman Percival Bower. (*Birmingham Central Library, Warwickshire Photographic Survey*)

Laying the foundation stone of the Valor Co. Ltd and Aston Brass Co. Ltd, Bromford Bridge, on 24 February 1925. Valor, manufacturers of gas appliances, still exist in the same area. *(Birmingham Central Library, Miscellaneous Collection)*

Cadbury workers relax in the grounds of the Bournville chocolate-making factory, listening to a midday concert, 1925. *(Birmingham Central Library, Miscellaneous Collection)*

Joseph Lucas Football Club, 1921. Many of the larger factories and offices had their own sporting facilities. Joseph Lucas, motor and cycle accessories manufacturers of Great King Street, was no exception. *(University of Birmingham, Chinn Collection)*

Herbert Austin seen at the wheel of an Austin 7, *c.* 1925. Austin, born at Little Missenden in Buckinghamshire, served an engineering apprenticeship in Australia and returned to England in 1890 where he worked for the Wolseley Sheep Shearing Company in Birmingham. Made a director in 1900 he then took control of the Wolseley Tool and Motor Company until 1905 when he began to make his own cars at Longbridge. The Austin 7 was one of the most popular cars he made. Austin died in 1941 aged seventy-four. *(Birmingham Central Library, Warwickshire Photographic Survey)*

Southalls, makers of surgical dressings as well as chemical apparatus, at Saltley. This shows girls cutting bandages, *c.* 1921. The company still exists today. *(Birmingham Central Library, Miscellaneous Collection)*

Small Heath Excelsior Cricket Club, 1926. This team had its headquarters in Joe Williams' coffee house on the Coventry Road and brought crowds to Saturday afternoon parks cricket. In the Birmingham Parks League this team got to Division One from Division Eight in five years. *(University of Birmingham, Chinn Collection)*

Handsworth Rugby Club, 1931/2. Another successful local sports club that had plenty of support. *(Simon Topman)*

Birmingham Public Libraries Book Exchange System, 1929. Note the fashion of the librarian and the style of the van. The original central library was opened in 1866, burned down in 1879, rebuilt in 1882 and remained in Ratcliff Place until the present building opened in 1973. The Book Exchange System was a method of obtaining required books from other libraries, now known as the Inter-Library Loan System. (*Birmingham Central Library, Warwickshire Photographic Survey*)

Spiceal Street from Jamaica Row, *c.* 1937. The railings of St Martin's in the Bull Ring can be seen on the right with the statue of Lord Nelson in the distance. On the left can be seen Woolworths and, further up, the entrance to the Market Hall whose interior was destroyed by an air raid in August 1940. Its exterior and most of this area were cleared in the early 1960s for the construction of the Bull Ring Shopping Centre. (*Birmingham Central Library, Warwickshire Photographic Survey*)

The Futurist Cinema, John Bright Street, 1928. A very popular cinema for many years, the first sound film *The Singing Fool* had its first showing here from 18 March to 11 May 1929. *(Birmingham Central Library, Warwickshire Photographic Survey)*

A portrait of Mr Ken Topman, jazz violinist and band leader, who broadcast regularly on BBC Radio in the 1930s. He was the owner of Topman's Ltd, a garage and motor car dealership (Rolls-Royce and Austin) on the corner of Holloway Head and Bristol Street then known as 'The Horse Fair'. *(Simon Topman)*

One of the most liked Hollywood stars of the 1930s, Gene Autry, the singing cowboy, brings New Street to a halt in a pre-war visit to the Odeon. *(University of Birmingham, Chinn Collection)*

Children from Peckham Road School, Kingstanding, on an outing to Lewis's Stores, Birmingham, in 1935 in order to purchase a pet rabbit. *(University of Birmingham, Chinn Collection)*

Party in Dartmouth Street celebrating the Silver Jubilee of King George V in 1935. Scenes like this were prevalent throughout Birmingham. *(Birmingham Central Library, Warwickshire Photographic Survey)*

The Queen Elizabeth Hospital, originally known as The Hospitals Centre, was opened in July 1938 by the Duke and Duchess of Gloucester. This photograph shows the building from the south-west in 1939. *(Birmingham Central Library, Warwickshire Photographic Survey)*

Construction of Baskerville House, 1939. In 1934 the City Council decided to erect a host of new municipal offices behind the Hall of Memory. Three years were to elapse before the approval was actually given. On 27 June 1938, the Lord Mayor, Councillor E.R. Canning, laid the foundation stone. The photograph shows the near completion of the East Wing of the Civic Centre as it appeared in July 1939. War and recession halted any further developments so this was the only building constructed. In March 1961 it was renamed 'Baskerville House' after the eighteenth-century printer who lived nearby. At present, staff from here are moving to Alpha Tower and elsewhere and Baskerville House is due to be converted into a luxury hotel. *(Birmingham Central Library, Warwickshire Photographic Survey)*

Birmingham University students dress up for their carnival day, 1936. (*Birmingham Central Library, Warwickshire Photographic Survey*)

On 11–14 July 1938, a pageant devised by Gwen Lally, tracing the city's history from earliest times, was held at Aston Park. It was a celebration to mark the centenary of Birmingham's incorporation as a borough and 6,000 performers were involved in the spectacular. These are 'Puritans' waiting to make their entrance. (*Birmingham Central Library, Warwickshire Photographic Survey*)

Decorations for the coronation of King George VI at the factory of Joseph Lucas, Great King Street, 1937. Following a complaint that decorations for the silver jubilee of King George V in 1935 were 'tawdry', Birmingham decided that, for the coronation of George VI, it would definitely improve its image. Specially appointed committees of the City Council and Chamber of Commerce began to work together and a comprehensive scheme was planned and put into execution by a single professional expert – William Haywood. (*Birmingham Central Library, Warwickshire Photographic Survey*)

An ox-roast in Harborne celebrating the coronation of King George VI on 12 May 1937. (*Birmingham Central Library, Warwickshire Photographic Survey*)

Mrs Alice Chambers being presented with a car she won for guessing the amount of money raised by the Birmingham University Carnival of 1932. Her husband, Mr William Sidney Chambers, is shown on the left. As the couple already owned a car the prize was bought back by the carnival committee. *(University of Birmingham, Chinn Collection)*

Results of a tornado which hit parts of Birmingham on 14 June 1931. The storm lasted for only four minutes but one woman was killed and many people were injured and made homeless. £50,000 worth of damage was caused. The worst hit areas were Small Heath, Bordesley Green, Sparkhill, Hall Green, Erdington and Greet. (*University of Birmingham, Chinn Collection*)

The Market Hall Clock, 1936. This magnificent clock is often remembered as being one of the wonders of Birmingham. It was made in 1883 by Messrs Potts of Leeds and was originally housed in the Imperial Arcade, Dale End. The Hall and the clock were destroyed in a Second World War air raid. The dial was 5 ft across, 18 sq ft in area and weighed 15 cwt. The largest bell weighed 3 cwt. The figures below represented Guy, Earl of Warwick, his wife, a retainer and a Saracen adversary. The two inner figures were over seven feet tall. (*Birmingham Central Library, Warwickshire Photographic Survey*)

Council meeting at Council House, Colmore Row, 1935. As usual in these meetings some people seem interested, others asleep. *(Birmingham Central Library, Warwickshire Photographic Survey)*

St Anne's Catholic School, Alcester Street, 1933. This school, founded by Cardinal John Henry Newman's Oratory priests in the late 1840s, has had a chequered history having moved to several sites. It was damaged by enemy action in 1940 and accommodation was provided for a short time in Moseley Road Council School. In 1947 the Junior and Infant department of St Michael's Roman Catholic School was transferred to repaired buildings of the closed Alcock Street Council School, and became an annexe of St Anne's. The school moved to a new site in Lowe Street in 1957. *(Birmingham Central Library, Warwickshire Photographic Survey)*

Corporation Street, 1939. Pedestrians ignore the safety precautions provided by a beacon crossing in Birmingham's busiest shopping thoroughfare. *(Birmingham Central Library, Miscellaneous Collection)*

Poolton's Fruit and Vegetable shop, Great Lister Street, *c.* 1935. A large and popular store close to where the University of Aston in Birmingham is now situated. Notice the number of fowl hanging from the rafters. *(Birmingham Central Library, Warwickshire Photographic Survey)*

As the threat of war loomed, the Birmingham-born Prime Minister, Neville Chamberlain, tried to prevent it. Here, the News Theatre in High Street in 1938 advertises its main film *Chamberlain the Peacemaker*. *(Birmingham Central Library, Warwickshire Photographic Survey)*

St Philip's Churchyard, 1939. A man in uniform and a woman walk through the grounds of St Philip's Cathedral possibly unaware that, within the next few days, their lives may change for ever with the announcement that the country 'is now at war with Germany'. *(Birmingham Central Library, Warwickshire Photographic Survey)*

The kitchen of a working class family in Kingstanding, *c.* 1932, taken by a well-known photographer – Bill Brandt. The conditions look sparse and primitive but were probably what most people had to live with during this period. *(Bournville Village Trust, Bill Brandt Collection)*

The Second World War and After

A story of what could be food rationing but is not. Olive Edwards holds Olive Brandreth while she rigs up a temporary front at 712 Coventry Road, Small Heath, following an incident when the shop was damaged, 28 October 1947. *(Birmingham Central Library, Miscellaneous Collection)*

As soon as war was declared gas masks were distributed across the country in case of dangerous fumes from incendiaries and bombs. Here, a group of Birmingham children try masks on for size on 2 October 1939. *(University of Birmingham, Chinn Collection)*

Thousands of city children across the country were evacuated to more rural areas immediately before and after the declaration of war. This group of Birmingham children were evacuated to the Stratford-upon-Avon area in October 1939. *(University of Birmingham, Chinn Collection)*

Petrol rationing, September 1939. A regular sight throughout the war as indeed was rationing of goods and produce in general. *(University of Birmingham, Chinn Collection)*

Birmingham ARP Ambulance Service drill, 1939. In 1938 an Air Raids Precaution Committee was elected as a standing committee of the City Council. Yet the invitation to local authorities and private employers to co-operate with the Government in setting up an ARP organisation, calling on the public to volunteer for duties and learn the rudiments of protection, had been issued three years earlier in July 1935. *(University of Birmingham, Chinn Collection)*

Birmingham nurses in wartime looking sprightly and happy, 1939. *(University of Birmingham, Chinn Collection)*

An ARP kitchen set up in Sparkhill to offer sustenance to volunteers, October 1939. *(University of Birmingham, Chinn Collection)*

Home Guard marching past the Council House, Colmore Row, *c*. 1940. *(Birmingham Post and Mail)*

Sparkbrook Home Guard, 1940. The Home Guard in Birmingham was split into two types – those attached to one of the City's thirty-five police stations or internal defence units of workers formed to protect their factories. The Sparkbrook guard are shown on the steps of the Carlton Cinema, Taunton Road. *(University of Birmingham, Chinn Collection)*

Remains of Anderson shelters at Oldnow Road, Small Heath, following an air raid, August 1940. *(Birmingham Central Library, Warwickshire Photographic Survey)*

ARPs helping to clear up in John Bright Street on 22 November 1940 following an air raid the previous night. *(Birmingham Central Library, Warwickshire Photographic Survey)*

Fire-fighters tackling a blaze following an air
attack on the High Street, looking towards the
Bull Ring, April 1940. *(Birmingham Central
Library, Warwickshire Photographic Survey)*

Fire-fighting at Holloway Head, October 1940.
(University of Birmingham, Chinn Collection)

Joe Lyons Café, Victoria Square, following an air raid in April 1941. The enemy appeared to have borne a grudge against the Lyons chain – several in Birmingham were destroyed. *(Birmingham Central Library, World War Two Collection)*

Waiting to see what damage has been done to the house and contents – trying to accept it without too many tears, August 1940. *(University of Birmingham, Chinn Collection)*

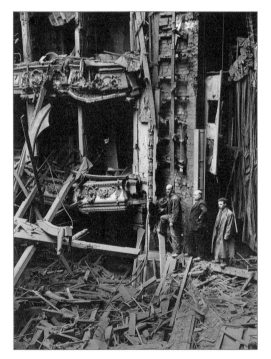

Damage to boxes and stage of the Prince of Wales Theatre, Broad Street, which was completely destroyed by bomb and fire damage on the night of 9/10 April 1941, making its managing director, Emile Littler, state 'It's finished for good and all'. This well-loved theatre had been erected as a music hall, intended to be used for high-class concerts, in 1856. It became licensed as a theatre in 1862 as the Royal Music Hall Operetta House and the Prince of Wales Operetta House in 1863, and shortly after the Prince of Wales Theatre. *(University of Birmingham, Chinn Collection)*

Members of Birmingham City Transport Home Guard, 31st and 32nd Warwickshire Birmingham Battalions, providing the Guard of Honour for the visit of Field Marshal Sir Bernard Montgomery on 9 March 1944. The officer at the rear of the photograph is believed to be Edward Poolton who worked for Birmingham City Transport. *(University of Birmingham, Chinn Collection)*

Surprise visit by King George VI following severe air raids. Here he talks to a group of residents in Queen's Road, *c.* 1941. *(University of Birmingham, Chinn Collection)*

In 1938 the decision was taken to open a massive factory between Fort Dunlop and Castle Bromwich airfield to make Spitfires. The Castle Bromwich 'Shadow Factory' was to be the largest in Britain covering 345 acres and employing 12,000 people. Here we see Spitfires and Lancaster bombers on the runway at Castle Bromwich, 1944. *(Birmingham Central Library, Warwickshire Photographic Survey)*

Lancaster Bomber Assembly 'B' Block at Castle Bromwich, 1943. *(Birmingham Central Library, Warwickshire Photographic Survey)*

Queueing for horse meat, *c.* 1945. Horse meat became, if not popular, at least a type of meat that was easier to obtain than others. Here, 'Cheval Meat Stores', not listed in any trade directory, but believed to have been along Dudley Road, opens its doors for customers, *c.* 1945. (*Birmingham Central Library, Warwickshire Photographic Survey*)

Getting back to normal after the war. This is the High Street showing some remnants of bomb damage, 1946. (*Birmingham Central Library, Warwickshire Photographic Survey*)

King George VI and Queen Elizabeth being met by the Lord Mayor, John Burman, on a visit to Birmingham, 11 May 1948. Members of the Lord Mayor's family being introduced to the royal couple are Elizabeth, John, Roseanne and Michael Burman. (*Birmingham Central Library, Warwickshire Photographic Survey*)

From Austerity to Plenty

Kings Norton 'Mop Fair', 1953. The 'Mop', still held on Kings Norton Green on the first Monday in October, dates back to 1616 when James I granted the rights for the area to hold a certain number of markets and fairs throughout the year. Now it is mainly a funfair but originally it was used for hiring staff – housemaids brought their buckets and mops in the hope that they would be offered a job. *(Birmingham Central Library, Warwickshire Photographic Survey)*

Day's Shoe Shop, New Street, *c.* 1950. This was a very long established shop which sold extremely high quality shoes. The faces of the ladies seem to suggest that life was still austere in the years immediately following the war and that the shoes, although desirable, were perhaps too expensive. (*Birmingham Central Library, Warwickshire Photographic Survey*)

Queue for coke at Windsor Street Gasworks during a fuel shortage, February 1951. (*Birmingham Central Library, Warwickshire Photographic Survey*)

Coronation Day, 2 June 1953. Street party at Dawlish Road, Selly Oak. Street parties celebrating the coronation of Elizabeth II were held up and down the country. This one included everyone in fancy dress and a football match between Mums and Dads which the Mums won 2–0. *(University of Birmingham, Chinn Collection)*

Mums football team at the Dawlish Road coronation party, 1953. *(University of Birmingham, Chinn Collection)*

83

End of sugar rationing, 27 September 1953. This photograph of a happy group of shoppers was taken in the shop of Mr D. Sealey at 89 Addison Road, Kings Heath, a few days after the end of sugar rationing. (*Birmingham Central Library, Warwickshire Photographic Survey*)

Portrait of an Asian gentleman, possibly an immigrant, taken by the Dyche studios, *c.* 1955. Ernest Dyche (1887–1973) was a self-taught photographer who opened his first studio in Bordesley Green around 1910, originally specialising in theatrical portraiture – producing photographs of music hall and variety turns who performed on the Birmingham stage. A few years later he opened a second studio on Moseley Road, Balsall Heath where eventually his son, Ernest Malcolm (1921–90), joined him. During the 1950s immigrants from the Caribbean and the Indian sub-continent arrived in the city and many visited the Moseley Road studio to have portraits made for their friends and relatives back home, a tradition which was to last twenty-five years. *(Birmingham Central Library, Dyche Collection)*

A wedding photograph taken by Dyche, *c.* 1954. *(Birmingham Central Library, Dyche Collection)*

Bus snarl-up in Digbeth High Street, 1953. Problems continued along this major route into Birmingham from the Stratford and Coventry Roads areas until the middle of the decade, when the street was widened. (*Birmingham Central Library, Warwickshire Photographic Survey*)

Digbeth High Street after road widening, 1955. (*Birmingham Central Library, Warwickshire Photographic Survey*)

Rock 'n' roll fever in the foyer of the Birmingham Hippodrome in the mid-1950s. This dance craze arrived in Britain through the film *The Blackboard Jungle* which featured Bill Haley and the Comets playing *Rock Around the Clock*. This, in turn, led to another film of that name and teenagers were accused of tearing up cinema seats in their frenzy to dance. *(University of Birmingham, Chinn Collection)*

Local singer Jill Embury with the Billy Walker Band at the Mecca Casino Ballroom, Corporation Street, 1958. Jill took singing lessons from 1955 and by 1958 had her first professional engagement with the Billy Walker Band. She eventually appeared on TV's *Opportunity Knocks*, received a recording contract and appeared on television with Ken Dodd. *(University of Birmingham, Chinn Collection)*

Sunnymead hostel for youths on probation, 1958. This was situated on Weoley Park Road and was run jointly by the Home Office and Birmingham Rotary Club as a home base for those on probation. Here, the Lord Mayor, Donald Johnstone, pays a visit. The greased hair styles were the rage of the day. *(Miss Margery Elliott)*

The last tram in Birmingham – No. 616 Steelhouse Lane to Erdington – made its final journey on 14 July 1953. *(Birmingham Central Library, Warwickshire Photographic Survey)*

The Age of
the Mini

Children gathered around a lamp post in Gee Street, Newtown, 1961. The buildings were later demolished and flats built in their place. (*University of Birmingham, Chinn Collection*)

BBC's *Come Dancing* programme at Birmingham's Locarno Ballroom, Hurst Street, *c.* 1960. *(University of Birmingham, Chinn Collection)*

Before the age of discos live music was a favourite form of entertainment particularly in dance halls/ballrooms. This photograph shows a local group, the Brian Pearson Band, with soloist Jill Embury, on the roof of the Tower Ballroom, Edgbaston, 1963. *(University of Birmingham, Chinn Collection)*

'Project Crusader.' Under the auspices of the Bournville Youth Project scheme, four young Cadbury employees motored to the Holy Land following the Crusaders' route. They were seen off by Mr Charles Cadbury in May 1962. The four can be seen on the right with Mr Cadbury and are: Reg Griffiths, Stefan White, Roger Evans and Nick Thompson. The base man, Mr J.D. Smith, stayed at home and can be seen on the left looking towards the camera. *(Mr J.D. Smith)*

'Mini' Trim Lines at Longbridge, 1963. Since its first appearance in 1959, the Mini rapidly became Britain's most popular car. Here the body of the Mini, having travelled the full length of the trim line, is fully equipped with windows, electrics, steering gear and seats. *(Austin Motor Company Press Office)*

New Street Railway Station, 1968. A railway station has existed on New Street since 1854. Building of the current one began in 1964 and was completed by 1967. *(Birmingham Central Library, Warwickshire Photographic Survey)*

The Duke of Edinburgh seen opening the new Bull Ring Shopping Centre in the presence of the Lord Mayor, Alderman Frank Price, 23 May 1964. The whole development of the area, which included the demolition of the old Market Hall, was constructed by J. Laing. (*Birmingham Central Library, Warwickshire Photographic Survey*)

Crowds of eager shoppers pouring into the Bull Ring Centre immediately after its official opening. (*Birmingham Central Library, Warwickshire Photographic Survey*)

Camp Hill Flyover, 1961. Opened on 16 October 1961, this flyover was intended as a temporary measure to take traffic to the Stratford road – it was to last for over twenty-five years. *(Birmingham Central Library, Warwickshire Photographic Survey)*

Lee Mount off Lee Bank Road, 1968. The flats are typical of the multi-storey rehousing idea that persisted through the 1960s with little thought to the effect high rise dwellings might have. The older houses to the left were later demolished. *(Anthony Spettigue)*

Birmingham children from various ethnic communities enjoying themselves in the pool of the Chamberlain Memorial fountain, June 1961. In the centre of the photograph can be seen the Central Library which was demolished in 1974 following the move into the current building in Chamberlain Square. To the left can be seen the edge of the Town Hall. (*Birmingham Central Library, Warwickshire Photographic Survey*)

A Decade of Change

Fashion conscious 'man about town' in the 1970s. This young man seems to have enjoyed having his photograph taken at the studio of Dyche in Moseley Road. *(Birmingham Central Library, Dyche Collection)*

Demolition of some of Birmingham's earliest municipal houses in Lawrence Street, June 1971. The first council scheme was a twenty-two house site on Ryder Street completed in September 1890, followed by an eighty-two house site in nearby Lawrence Street completed in 1891. Rents were between 5*s* (25p) and 7*s* 6*d* (38p). Parts of the University of Aston in Birmingham are now situated in Lawrence Street. *(Birmingham Central Library, Warwickshire Photographic Survey)*

Demolition of the Church of the Messiah, Broad Street, April 1978. This large gothic church, designed by J.J. Bateman and built on arches over the Birmingham Canal, reflects the importance of the Unitarians in Birmingham, particularly in the latter half of the nineteenth century. It was the spiritual home of the Chamberlain and Nettlefold families. *(Birmingham Central Library, Warwickshire Photographic Survey)*

Gem Street School, 1973. This school was originally opened in 1888 as a girls' school for children who were too poor and dirty for ordinary Board Schools. A bath was provided at the school and within a year very good results in health and appearance were reported. A school for deaf children was built on the site in 1900. The building was altered in 1901 for boys who were transferred from Staniforth Street Board School. Later it was used for deaf children again. *(Birmingham Central Library, Warwickshire Photographic Survey)*

Polytechnic demonstration, October 1974. Students from Birmingham Polytechnic demonstrate over the cuts in educational spending which regularly occurred during the decade. *(Birmingham Central Library, Warwickshire Photographic Survey)*

Rush hour traffic, 1971. A winter's night whirl of cars along Lichfield Road before the Aston Expressway was opened. *(Birmingham Central Library, Warwickshire Photographic Survey)*

Gravelly Hill interchange, 1972. Usually known as 'Spaghetti Junction' this was the engineering wonder of its age when it first opened in 1972. It forms the hub of Britain's motorway system and took away the streams of traffic from what were then ordinary roads. *(Birmingham Central Library, Warwickshire Photographic Survey)*

Resting after a hard day's shopping, 1973.
Street furniture such as these seats have
been available in the city since the 1970s
and provide a welcome relief for those who
have been walking their feet off at the shops.
(Birmingham Central Library, Warwickshire
Photographic Survey)

Crescent Wharf, 1976. The areas surrounding Birmingham's canal systems have undergone much restoration
since the '70s and now provide a haven of peace for those who may wish to amble, take a canal boat ride
or simply relax in one of the many pubs and cafés that have sprung up along Gas Street and Brindley Place.
Crescent Wharf was one of the first to be improved in such a way but has changed yet again because of
Brindley Place. *(Birmingham Central Library, Warwickshire Photographic Survey)*

Balsall Heath, 1970. This evocative photograph shows that near penury was still a problem for families as late as the 1970s, but it does not dampen the love for lesser species as the boy's gentleness towards the pigeon shows in the way he handles it. *(Alan Wood)*

St Paul's School, Balsall Heath, 1976. This school began as an independent one set up by parents for children who regularly played truant and its first class was held in someone's living room. It is now housed in its own building, employs professional teachers and is grant maintained. The school also now forms part of a multi-faceted social and educational group known as the St Paul's Community Project Ltd. Here, the first students pose for a photograph outside the original school premises. *(St Paul's Community Project)*

Queen's Silver Jubilee, 1977. The Queen visited the city as part of her Silver Jubilee celebrations in 1977. Here, crowds opposite the Hall of Memory wait to catch a glimpse of her as she presents new colours to the 2nd Battalion Mercian Volunteers. *(Birmingham Central Library, Warwickshire Photographic Survey)*

Queen's Silver Jubilee, 1977. The Queen enters the Metropole Hotel at the National Exhibition Centre where she is to dine as part of her day in Birmingham. *(Birmingham Post and Mail)*

Fire at Lotus Shoe Shop, New Street, 1970. A dramatic photograph showing the local fire brigade at work. *(Birmingham Central Library, Warwickshire Photographic Survey)*

The Emergence
of Service

Sikh service in Chamberlain Square, June 1984. Many hundreds of Sikhs attended this short service which followed a peaceful walk through the city in memory of those killed at Amritsar earlier in the month. *(Birmingham Central Library, Warwickshire Photographic Survey)*

The Aston Hippodrome, a favourite Birmingham theatre that came to the end of its life in the 1980s. One of the most famous performers reputed to have appeared here regularly, was Charlie Chaplin who is supposed to have spent most of his time in the Barton's Arms public house situated almost directly opposite the theatre. *(Birmingham Central Library, Warwickshire Photographic Survey)*

Renovations to Birmingham Hippodrome, 1980. Often regarded as Birmingham's premier theatre, the Hippodrome has undergone many alterations and renovations over the years. After the show *Elvis – The Musical* ended in July 1980 the theatre closed. It reopened in the following year when more than £2,000,000 had been spent improving backstage and completely refurbishing the auditorium. *(Birmingham Central Library, Warwickshire Photographic Survey)*

Chamberlain Square, 1982. Here, the Chamberlain Memorial and Square had not long undergone restoration after a successful fund raising exercise organised by the Birmingham Civic Society. Today the area is not as tranquil as this. Throughout the year entertainers of all descriptions can be found attracting crowds of passers by. (*Birmingham Central Library, Warwickshire Photographic Survey*)

107

Restoration work to 'Big Brum', 1982. A rather unusual view of the famous clock as it undergoes a revamp. (*Birmingham Central Library, Warwickshire Photographic Survey*)

Corporation Street ready for the Rotary convention. June 1984 saw the invasion of over 20,000 Rotarians at the first International Rotary Convention to be held in the UK since 1921 – the last being in the Usher Hall, Edinburgh. The Birmingham event was held at the National Exhibition Centre but accommodation was spread out in a sixty mile radius in every direction. (*Birmingham Central Library, Warwickshire Photographic Survey*)

Bingley Hall, 1981. This exhibition hall, designed by Julius Alfred Chatwin, was constructed in 1850 and was then the largest building in Birmingham, enclosing an area of 1.25 acres and capable of accommodating 25,000 people. It opened with the Birmingham Cattle Show, the first of a varied programme of exhibitions and events to be held there. *(Birmingham Central Library, Warwickshire Photographic Survey)*

Demolition of Bingley Hall, 1984. Bingley Hall was partly damaged by fire in January 1984 and, by June of that year, had been completely demolished. The last show to be exhibited was the International Custom and Sports Car Show. *(Birmingham Central Library, Warwickshire Photographic Survey)*

Foundation stone laying, 30 October 1986. Jacques Delors, the then President of the European Community, laid the foundation stone for the prestigious International Convention Centre at Broad Street. To the right can be seen the Lord Mayor, Councillor Denis Martineau and his consort, Mrs Mollie Martineau. (*Birmingham Central Library, Warwickshire Photographic Survey*)

International Convention Centre, 1989. Here the construction is well under way. It was built on the site of the former exhibition area – Bingley Hall – and the new centre was opened in June 1991 by HRH the Queen. (*Birmingham Central Library, Warwickshire Photographic Survey*)

Steam-powered narrowboat, 1984. This was the last surviving steam-powered narrowboat and is seen on the canal beneath Newhall Street, close to the former Museum of Science and Industry. The boat was built at Saltley in 1909 by Fellows, Morton and Clayton. *(Birmingham Central Library, Warwickshire Photographic Survey)*

Motor racing in Birmingham, 1986. In May 1971, former racing driver and managing director of the Opposite Lock club, Martin Hone, together with Neville Borg, City Engineer and Surveyor, submitted plans to the Council for staging a 'Monaco-style' road race through the streets of Birmingham. It was to take another fifteen years before such an event was staged and, in 1986, August Bank holiday Sunday and Monday were the two days selected for the Formula 3000 and supporting races, the former being one step down from Formula 1. The event became known as the Birmingham Super Prix. The photograph shows 180 mph action on the streets as Formula 3000 roar down Belgrave Middleway. (*Birmingham Central Library, Warwickshire Photographic Survey*)

Centenary of Birmingham, 1989. On 13 January 1989 Birmingham celebrated its centenary as a city with numerous events including an enactment of a visit to the city by Queen Victoria. (She didn't actually come in 1889.) Thousands of people lined the streets and these are some of the revellers outside the Council House. (*Birmingham Central Library, Warwickshire Photographic Survey*)

Forward to the Millennium

The *Iron Man*, 1993. One half of Anthony Gormley's sculpture, the *Iron Man* being manoeuvred at Firth Rixson Castings Ltd, Willenhall. The piece was commissioned by the TSB bank and donated to the City of Birmingham as part of its policy for encouraging public sculpture. It was unveiled in 1993 outside the then offices of the TSB at the top end of New Street between Pinfold and Hill Streets and has never failed to be controversial, although most 'Brummies' view it with great affection. *(Anthony Gormley and Rod Dorling)*

Demonstration in Chamberlain Square begging politicians to stop the war in the Gulf, 1992. *(Roger Joyce)*

The attack of the dragon, 1991. Children pretend to be frightened and run away from an attacking 'dragon', in one of the many celebrations to be held regularly in Centenary Square. *(Roger Joyce)*

Thomas Attwood (1783–1856) and friends. This statue, shown reclining on the steps of Chamberlain Square, is of the well-known agitator for Parliamentary Reform and Birmingham's first Member of Parliament. The statue was designed and sculpted by Sioban Coppinger and Fiona Peever and unveiled in 1993. The statue was commissioned and donated by Mrs Patricia Mitchell, the great-great-granddaughter of Thomas Attwood. *(Keith Harris)*

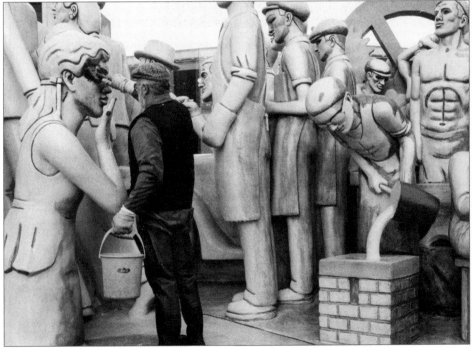

Cleaning *Forward* in Centenary Square, 1992. Unveiled in 1991 this sculpture, created by Birmingham-born Raymond Mason, is made from fibre-glass and painted in cream and pink. It is often greeted with derision and indifference but it stands optimistic and proud. It takes as its theme the advancement of Birmingham people through the centuries and includes characters of well-known locals including Joseph Chamberlain and Josiah Mason as well as general artisans and workers. *(Keith Harris)*

115

Model for 'Floozie in the Jacuzzi'. May 1993 saw the unveiling by the Princess of Wales of a vast sculptural project. The project designed by Dhriva Mistry links the upper level in front of the Council House with a stepped water feature to New Street below. It is officially called *River, Youth, Guardians and Object (Variations)* but the part situated directly in front of the Council House, *The River*, is affectionately known as 'The Floozie in the Jacuzzi'. The photograph shows a model of *The River*. (*Birmingham Central Library, Colmore Row Collection*)

International Convention Centre, 1991. View of the Centre together with Symphony Hall, Birmingham Repertory Theatre to the right with Centenary Square (named in a competition held in Birmingham's centenary year, 1989) with the statue *Forward* front right. *(Birmingham Central Library, Warwickshire Photographic Survey)*

Walking through the International Convention Centre, 1991. To the left is the entrance to Symphony Hall and to the right are the Convention Centre halls. *(Birmingham Central Library, Warwickshire Photographic Survey)*

Symphony Hall, 1991. This huge concert hall, now the home of the Birmingham Symphony Orchestra and venue for international stars of both classical and popular music, was officially opened with a gala concert on 12 June 1991. HRH the Princess Royal was in attendance, although the first concert had been held a few weeks previously on 15 April. The hall is now considered by public, musicians and critics as one of the finest, if not *the* finest, concert venue in the world. *(Birmingham Central Library, Warwickshire Photographic Survey)*

Concert in Symphony Hall, 1992. *(Birmingham Central Library, Warwickshire Photographic Survey)*

Canal cruises outside the International Convention Centre, 1991. Since the opening of the ICC, cruises along the Birmingham Canal have proved to be extremely popular with residents and visitors. Sights to be seen include the National Indoor Arena, Sea World and the revamped Gas Street Basin in which, if lucky, people can view many colourful narrowboats in dock. (*Birmingham Central Library, Warwickshire Photographic Survey*)

Canal cruising outside the National Indoor Arena, 1991. The National Indoor Arena was opened on 4 October 1991 by Dr Primo Nebiolo, the then president of the International Amateur Athletics Federation. The Arena had already achieved fame, even before the doors were open, because of its 200 metre, six lane track that could be assembled for athletic events and then stored when not required. It was the first track of its type in the United Kingdom and said to be one of the fastest in the world. The arena also achieved fame as the place where the television programme *Gladiators* was recorded.

The Glance. Rock in the heart of Birmingham in St Philip's Churchyard, 1991. *(Roger Joyce)*

Acknowledgements

Birmingham Central Library, *Birmingham Post and Mail*, Bournville Village Trust, Dr Carl Chinn, Rod Dorling, Margery Elliott, Anthony Gormley, Keith Harris, Roger Joyce, St Paul's Community Project, Jean Smith, John Smith, Anthony Spettigue, Simon Topman, University of Birmingham, John Whybrow Ltd, Alan Wood.

Panoramic view of Birmingham, 1973. *(Birmingham Central Library, Warwickshire Photographic Survey)*